Scotland Amazing Pictures & Fun Facts (Kid Kongo Travel The World Series) (Book 10)

Kid Kongo

D1400361

Other Books By Kid Kongo

TRAVEL THE WORLD SERIES

1. SEDONA
2. ALASKA
3. AFRICA
4. CALIFORNIA
5. ARIZONA
6. I GREW UP ON MY COMPUTER
7. THE DIABOLICAL EVIL GENIUS CAT THAT WANTED TO STEAL CHRISTMAS AND BECOME SANTA.
8. POLAND
9. SHAPES: FOR 3 TO 6 YEAR OLDS
10. GERMANY

MANY MORE.....

SCOTLAND

Scotland is part of Great Britain. It is made up of 790 islands and part of the northern part of England. It lies next to the Atlantic Ocean. Edinburgh is the capital of Scotland. In the European Union in which it is part of it contains the largest oil reserves.

IN MY DEFENS GOD ME DEFEND

"In My Defense God Me Defend," is the country motto. Scotland comes from the latin word scotia which means land of the Gaels. For a brief period it was though of as Ireland, but around the mid century or 11 hundreds it became know as scotland and was the common name for it in the middle ages.

Scottish BagPipes

Scottish music has its own sound. Traditionally around the world Scottish bag pipes are well known for there distinct three drone melody that are blown with an air bag. Unknown from the world the fiddle and accordion are also traditional Scottish instruments.

Sports

In Scotland sports have been a major part of there culture since the 16th cenutry. In fact the oldest national trophy in the entire world is the Scottish Cup for football (soccer in United States). The earliest history of soccer being played in Scotland dates back to 1424. Golf was first played in Scotland in the 15th century and is the birth place of Golf. Scotland hosted the worlds first and oldest golf tournaments called, " The Open Championship." Scotland is also known for the Highland games with the caber toss, stone put, hammer throw, weight throw, weight over bar, Sheaf toss, and Maide Lesig.

THE NATiONAL SYMBOL:

The unicorn is the national symbol of Scotland and has been the symbol since the 12th century. The climate in Scotland changes from cool, to hot, to wet summers, to cold winters. It is located near the ocean around 55, 57 N to 3, 11 degree west. Because if its northern location and atlantic sea trade winds causes the varying degree of climate changes year round..

Scotland's Double Jeopardy Act of 2011

Scotland's leagel system is that based on Roman rule and comparable tot he English and United States Justice System. One new difference now is that they have enacted a double jeopardy clause. Before if someone was fond not guilty and later evidence or admittance proved that they were, they couldn't be retried for the same crime and thus got away with the crime. Now if new evidence emerges or person admits to it after being found not guilty they can now go back to court and face charges again for the crime.

The Treaty OF York

The treaty of York established the separation between England and Scotland. It was established on September 25, 1237 between Henry the Third of England and Alexander the second of Scotland. The Scottish kind was attempting to move his land further southward into the English land. This established the barrier between the two kingdoms with the Treaty of York.

OLDEST LiViNG TREE

Europe's oldest living tree is the Grand Fir that is planted beside the area of Loch'e Fine and the Forting Yew which are said to be over 5,000 years old.

SCOTLAND EDUCATION

Scotland has some of the most high and respected Universities in the World, some among the oldest in the World. The University of St Andrew, the University of Glasgow, the University of Aberdeen, the University of Edinburgh, and the University of Dundee. In 2014 it was shown by the Office of National Statistics that Scotland has the highest of age 16 to 64 at a NVQ 4 level and above.

SCOTTiSH FOOD

If you visit Scotland there are many Fish and Chips and fast food shops that have taken root into the culture. Traditional dishes in Scotland known around the world are Haggis, smoked salmon, boiled gigot, game soup, howtowdie with Drappit eggs, Kilmeny Kail,, stoppage, and many more.

SCOTTiSH CLANS

Scottish clans, clan being gaelic for children were groups of Scottish people that had their own tartan patterns in klts, clothing , and crest. Modern thought of clans are actually misconceived and often clans aren't related by blood at all. Back in the ages when there were clans in Scotland the people who were beneath a chieftains and lived in his community under his protection would take the chiefs last name. This was common in the 16th and early 17th century.

GLASGOW SCOTLAND

Glasgow is the largest city in Scotland. It is located at the banks of the River Clyde. It has around 2 million people that live in the greater Glasgow Urban area. Glasgow along with all of Scotland is predominately made up of caucasians.

HEALTHCARE

Scotland has there own healthcare founded by the national health service act of 1947. Prescriptions are free , but if you make a certain amount of money in Scotland you can be charged by dentist and doctors. The life expectancy in Scotland is pretty good. For males it is around 77 years old and females it is 80 years old.

MILITARY

Scotland is part of the British armed forces. They include the Scots Guards, the Royal Scots Dragoon Guards and the Scot Regiment, the Royal Logistic Corps. Since Scotland is such a remote place there are many military facilities from England that are located there. Even the Open-Air live depleted Uranium weapons test are done on a Scottish island that is isolated.

ANiMALS

Scotland has many species of wildlife. These animals include ptarmigan, mountain hare, stout, golden eagle, gannets. These are widespread across England and some parts of Europe. It also has a rich bryophyte flora that is important for the world.

TRANSPORTS

Scotland has five main airports located in Glasglow, Edinburgh, Aberdeen, Prestwick, and inverness. Then there are 11 regional airports located throughout Scotland. Scotland also has a rail network managed by Transport Scotland. About 40,000 people use the subway system in Scotland and is set to have more improvements done to it.

Languages

Scotland has 3 languages that it officially recognizes. English, Scots, and Scottish Gaelic. Gaelic is usually a language mostly spoken on the tiny islands in the wester Isles, but only around 1 percent of the people actually speak the language.

Castles In Scotland

About The Author:

Kid Kongo is a children's book and song writer that believes education is the key to success. This is part of the Travel the World series. When not traveling, touring, writing, photographing, web designing, and illustrating he lives in the sticks in Arizona.

Made in the USA
Middletown, DE
14 October 2016